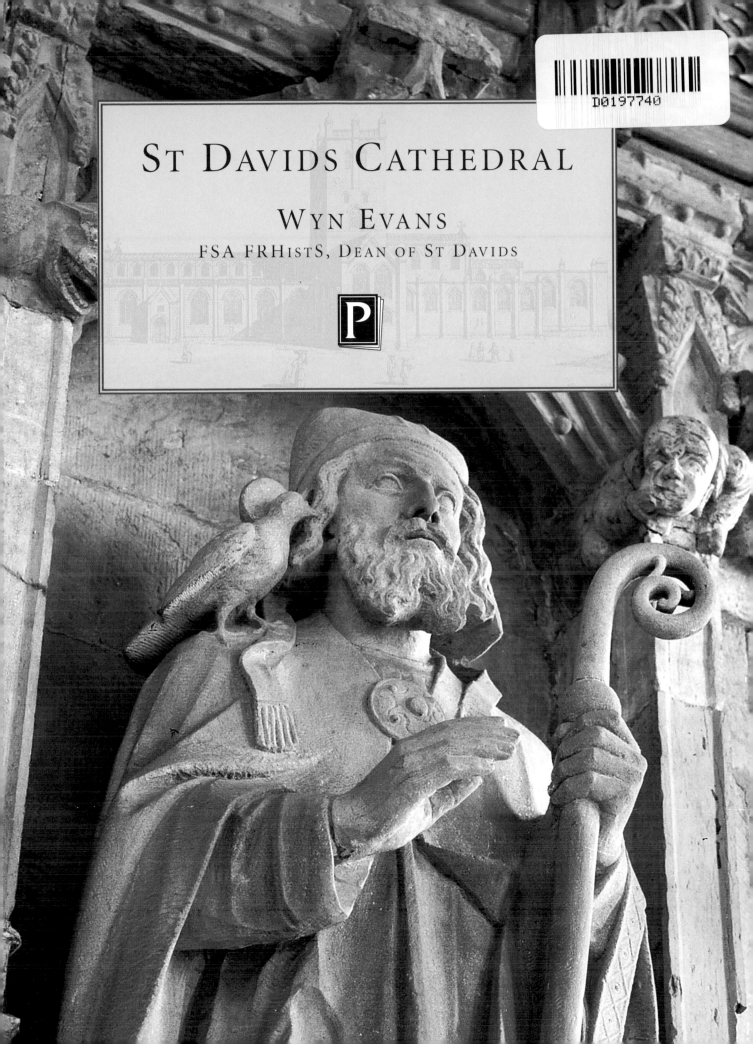

St Davids Cathedral

Wyn Evans

FSA FRHistS, Dean of St Davids

Edited by John McIlwain.
Designed by Simon Borrough.

All photography (by Peter Smith of Newbery Smith Photography, and
Philip Clarke) copyright © St Davids Cathedral, except:
Philip Clarke: p.38 top, p.83, pp.84–85; C.R.A. Davies FRCP: p.11,
p.12, p.13, p.25, p.32, p.42, p.43, p.45, p.47 centre, pp.68–9, p.73,
p.76, p.78, back flap; Pembrokeshire County Library: p.57 top;
Jarrold Publishing: p.6, p.17, p.18, p.22, p.24, pp.36–7, p.38 bottom,
p.42, p.47 top, p.53, p.56, p.60, p.62 top, p.64, p.66, p.67 main, p.68
bottom left, p.70, pp.70–1, p.72 top, p.84 bottom; Patrick Lichfield:
p.82; John McIlwain: p.9 top; Skyscan: p.39; Chris Warren
Photography: p.7.

The map of the Close on the inside back cover was created by Martin
Stancliffe Architects and is used with their kind permission.

A CIP catalogue record for this book is available from the British
Library.

Published by:
Jarrold Publishing
Healey House, Dene Road, Andover, Hampshire, SP10 2AA
Sales: 01264 409206
Enquiries: 01264 409200
Fax: 01264 334110
e-mail: heritagesales@jarrold.com
website: www.britguides.com

Set in Minion.
Printed in Singapore.   1/02

ISBN 1 84165 098 6

Pitkin Guides is an imprint of Jarrold Publishing, Norwich.

▶ FROM THE SOUTH PORCH, A
FIGURE OF BASIL JONES, BISHOP OF
ST DAVIDS 1874–97, JOINT
AUTHOR OF THE CLASSIC VICTO-
RIAN STUDY OF THE CATHEDRAL.

CONTENTS

ST DAVIDS: THE SETTING

St Davids Cathedral lies at the west end of Wales, on a peninsula thrusting out into the Atlantic. Although on today's map the area looks isolated, at the time of *Dewi Sant* (St David) it was pivotal. At the junction of a major land route and significant sea routes, the peninsula formed, in effect, a bridge to Ireland, Scotland and north-west Britain, and also afforded access to Cornwall, and thence to Brittany and the Continent. Thus, it seems that David and his contemporaries chose western Britain for their monastic settlements not just, as one might suppose, to get away from it all, but rather to be at the centre of things.

Sea meets land here, and the landscape is harsh; high, hard, ancient rocks thrown up by ancient cataclysms rear up on to the horizon. Near the western end of the peninsula, where the geology is at its most complex, the River Alun has gouged a small, fairly deep, valley. Here, sheltered from the Atlantic gales, lies St Davids Cathedral. It was here, or so it is believed, that David came with his monks, some time in the middle of the 6th century. He chose for his monastery the sort of place that nobody else wanted, poorly drained and overgrown. Both Latin names for St Davids emphasize this: *Vallis Rosina* means 'the valley of the little swamp'; *Menevia* means a thicket or brushwood.

It is thought that David sited his monastery, (which, of course, was nothing like the present cathedral), on the higher, drier part of the site, at a bend in the river near a spring. Legend has it that this was discovered through David's striking the ground with his staff during a dry summer. The spring still exists, as does the well which was built over it, but just as the probable site of the monastery is covered by the present presbytery, so the well lies concealed beneath the ground outside the Lady Chapel.

There were also likely political and ecclesiastical reasons for David's choice of location. Given that the sea was more highway than barrier in his time, there were strong cultural and political links between Ireland and Wales. The dynasty which then ruled the kingdom of Dyfed (which included St Davids), had its origins in south-east Ireland. Indeed, the whole ambience of both Dewi's life and the site associated with him has an Irish tinge even to its name, the Irish *muine* from which Menevia derived. There is also a strong Irish flavour and connections expressed in the Life of David. Ironically, David's own descent was from Cunedda, the Welsh leader who is thought to have expelled the Irish from North Wales.

From these very small, apparently remote, beginnings grew not just a medieval cathedral – magnificent, large, European as it is – but also an important centre, the focus of the cult of David which ultimately became that of the patron saint of Wales.

▲ ST DAVIDS CATHEDRAL LIES NEAR THE COAST IN THE VALLEY OF THE RIVER ALUN. RAMSEY ISLAND, BEYOND, IS ALSO KNOWN AS 'YNYS DEWI', (THE ISLAND OF DAVID).

▼ THE ANCIENT ROCKS OF ST DAVIDS PENINSULA. AT THE TIME OF DAVID THE PENINSULA, FAR FROM BEING ISOLATED, STOOD AT AN IMPORTANT 'CROSSROADS' BETWEEN LAND ROUTES FROM CENTRES OF POPULATION IN MAINLAND ENGLAND AND SEA ROUTES TO IRELAND, SCOTLAND, CORNWALL AND FRANCE.

DAVID, PATRON SAINT AND FOUNDER

It has to be said at the outset that very little is known about David. He is thought to have died in a year when 1st March fell on a Tuesday, but this could have been either AD 589 or 602. The Life of David, the *Vita*, is the earliest life of a Welsh saint to survive, written in the 11th century by Rhigyfarch, son of Sulien, a bishop of St Davids. It was, however, written about 500 years after David's death, and is clearly coloured by the circum-

stances of the time. The Normans were pushing heavily into western Wales and the Life clearly sets out to show that the Church in Wales had antiquity, orthodoxy, austerity and sainthood to match anything the Normans could introduce.

Tradition says that David was born on the cliffs about 1¹/₂ miles (3 kilometres) to the south of the cathedral, where the present ruined St Non's Chapel

▼ THE CATHEDRAL FROM THE NORTH. DAVID BUILT HIS MONASTERY ON A RELATIVELY DRY BUT OTHERWISE UNFORGIVING PART OF THE VALLEY. TODAY'S MEDIEVAL CATHEDRAL BEARS NO PHYSICAL RESEMBLANCE TO THE ORIGINAL MONASTIC COMMUNITY.

stands today, Non, or Nonnita, being David's mother. However, there are place names elsewhere in south-west Wales which express connections both with Dewi and Non. The core of the cult of David appears to be in the Aeron and the Teifi valleys in Ceredigion. It is therefore possible that the cult may have shifted from there to where St Davids is now. On the other hand, the reverse may have been true. In the 10th and 11th centuries,

▶ AN EARLY CHRISTIAN MONUMENT IN THE RUINED CHAPEL OF ST NON, SOUTH OF ST DAVIDS. HERE, LEGEND HAS IT, DAVID WAS BORN.

Viking raiders destroyed Menevia several times, in the process killing two bishops, Morgenau in 999 and Abraham in 1080. The community may therefore have had to move David's relics from place to place, perhaps including the Ceredigion sites. Indeed, at one point in the early 11th century, St Davids itself appears to have been abandoned.

Certainly, from the later 11th century, the idea developed that David had been born in the area, as did the traditions that local place names reflected incidents in his life and ministry. For example, to the west of the cathedral lies *Clegyr Boia*, (the rock of Boia). Boia was a local chieftain who, legend has it, objected to David's arrival. The smoke from David's fires was a sign that he had occupied the land without permission – permission that, as a pagan, Boia was unlikely to grant, even though the valley was marshy and Dewi the son of a prince. Both Boia and his wife tried to move him out, unsuccessfully as it seems. According to legend, fire from heaven came down and consumed the chieftain, his family and his citadel.

By the high Middle Ages, there existed in the area a sacred landscape of churches linked to the life and miracles of David, and those of other saints, including the chapels of St Patrick, St Justinian, St Non and the Chapel of the Fathom *(Capel y Gwrhyd)*. Patrick, according to the Life of David, was warned by angels to leave for Ireland 30 years before David's birth, to allow David to settle and found his monastery. The ruins of St Patrick's Chapel above Whitesands Bay, badly excavated in the 1920s, have almost completely disappeared under the sands. Other place names associated with Patrick in that area suggest that David's monastery might originally have been located there. Justinian, so tradition has it, was David's confessor. The relics of the two saints were held together in the great medieval shrine before its destruction. St Justinian's Chapel, at the little harbour bearing his name, is a roofless, early 16th-century building which, like St Patrick's Chapel, overlies an earlier chapel and too has been covered by sand once more. The Chapel of the Fathom is also linked to David. There was said to have been a figure on the wall with arms outstretched in a six-foot (2-metre)

span – that is, a fathom. The chapel has disappeared completely, although parts of it survive, built into the modern version of St Non's Chapel, which stands on the cliffs near its ruined counterpart.

David's birth appears, to say the least, to have been irregular, in that he was the result of a rape committed by his father, Sant, on Non, the daughter of a local chieftain. Both Non and David became 'water people': those whose attempt to live the Christian life led them to an existence of extreme self-deprivation, surviving on bread and water alone, and frequently standing up to the neck in water for hours in order to subdue any urges of the flesh. The body counted for nothing – the spirit was everything.

According to the Life of David, the monastic community lived in similar austerity. A man wishing to join, after being kept outside for a considerable time, would be received naked, as if in a shipwreck. Within the monastery, life did not get any easier, because David refused to use draught animals. Rather, his monks had to put the yoke on their own shoulders to plough the fields. They lived on bread, herbs and water – no meat, which was considered to fuel fleshly lusts, thus damaging the spiritual life.

Time was spent in four main ways: toiling in the fields, in church services, in private prayer and in study. However, there is some debate as to whether Rhigyfarch's description is authentic, for such an ascetic way of life was not characteristic of the mainstream Welsh Church in the 11th century, when he was writing. Two characteristics of David's regime survived long after his death. One of these was vegetarianism. Records show that Bishop Morgenau's death in 999, at the hands of the Vikings, was seen to be a judgement, as he was said to have been the first to eat meat since the time of David. The second was the quality of learning. When King Alfred needed someone to help him rebuild intellectual life in Wessex after the Vikings, he sought out Asser, Bishop of St Davids and later Bishop of Sherborne.

A true assessment of David is not easy. His life-denying behaviour is difficult to understand today, yet undoubtedly when he was alive people flocked here to seek his counsel. After his death, they prayed at the

▲ THE MODERN STATUE FROM THE SCREEN HAS ST DAVID
ANACHRONISTICALLY DRESSED AS A NORMAN BISHOP. A DOVE IS
SAID TO HAVE DESCENDED TO THE SAINT'S SHOULDER AFTER HIS
ADDRESS TO THE SYNOD OF BISHOPS AT LLANDDEWI BREFI.

tomb for his intercession on their behalf; and they sought burial close to him, in order to have a better chance on the day of judgement. David is supposed to have been very tall, but nothing survives to tell of what he looked like. All representations of him in the cathedral and elsewhere are modern. One enduring image shows him with a dove on his shoulder. This refers to an incident in the Life where he went, reluctantly, to address a synod of bishops at Llanddewi Brefi in the Teifi valley. But, out of doors, few of the large crowd could hear him. So, says the Life, a boy put a handkerchief on the ground before him. David stepped onto it, at which the ground rose beneath him, forming a little hill. Now everyone could hear, and so eloquently did he speak that the Holy Spirit, symbolized by a dove, came and rested on his shoulder. Llanddewi Brefi is a very important 'David site'. Built into a wall of the church are fragments of an inscription which is the first reference to him, on an early medieval tombstone of one Idnerth, son of James, 'who was killed on account of the property of David', probably in defending it.

David lived in the 6th century, the so-called 'age of the saints', and a period when many monasteries were being founded. The monastery at St Davids, like many others, became rich and famous. Yet nothing of it remains today. There are two main reasons for this. Firstly, the community of monks and theological students would have lived in huts of wood, mud or stone, with perhaps nearby a small oratory, a refectory, a cross and a cemetery. None of these simple structures would have survived the climate indefinitely, but this fact was not put to the test for, from the 7th century onwards, the settlement was subject to repeated burning and looting by seaborne raiders and others. Indeed, so complete was the destruction, it is said that an 11th-century priest seeking the tomb of the saint took a week to cut his way through the undergrowth which had amassed around it.

Yet, there are some survivals from the pre-Norman period. In the lapidarium are most of the ancient stones which have been found on or near the cathedral. Only two of these are closely provenanced. They were found when the Lady Chapel was being restored in the

19th century and are now in the cathedral exhibition in the Porth-y-Twr. One is part of a 10th-century grave slab which had two six-winged seraphs on it, of which one survives. Much more important is the so-called Abraham stone, the gravestone of the sons of Bishop Abraham. Of considerable historical interest, it shows that the pre-Norman Church in Wales had no problems about clerical, or even episcopal marriage. In fact, there was a very strong family interest in most of the major churches at that point. Very few examples of handwriting from the pre-Norman Church in Wales have survived, even on manuscript, which makes the stone's inscription remarkable. Finally, the stone has two kinds of cross carved on it, Celtic and Latin, which reflect the influence of continental ideas coming in with the Normans.

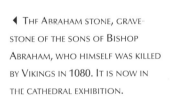

◀ PART OF A 10TH-CENTURY GRAVE SLAB, FOUND DURING RESTORATION OF THE LADY CHAPEL, NOW DISPLAYED IN THE EXHIBITION IN PORTH-Y-TWR. ONE OF A PAIR OF SIX-WINGED SERAPHS IS VISIBLE TOP LEFT.

◀ THE ABRAHAM STONE, GRAVE-STONE OF THE SONS OF BISHOP ABRAHAM, WHO HIMSELF WAS KILLED BY VIKINGS IN 1080. IT IS NOW IN THE CATHEDRAL EXHIBITION.

▶ THIS MODERN STATUE OF DAVID IN LLANDDEWI BREFI CHURCH BEARS MORE RESEMBLANCE TO THE SAINT'S LIKELY APPEARANCE THAN THE IMAGES IN THE CATHEDRAL, CONSID-ERING THE DRESS OF HIS ERA AND THE AUSTERITY OF HIS EXISTENCE.

◀ THIS VIEW FROM THE SOUTH SHOWS CLEARLY BISHOP GOWER'S HEIGHTENED NAVE AISLE (LEFT) AND THE TOWER, PRESBYTERY AND SOUTH TRANSEPT RESTORED BY SIR GEORGE GILBERT SCOTT.

▼ FINE 16TH-CENTURY ENCAUSTIC TILES RELAID IN THE SANCTUARY BY SCOTT DURING HIS RESTORATION.

BUILDING THE CATHEDRAL: BISHOP BERNARD

The Normans arrived in Wales towards the end of the 11th century, William the Conqueror himself coming to St Davids in 1081. The Welsh-Latin Chronicle kept at St Davids until the 13th century says that he came to pray, which is plausible, but a more pressing reason for his visit was his fear of invasion from Ireland, given its proximity. This fear may have been kindled by an event of that same year. Gruffydd ap Cynan, king of Gwynedd (North Wales), who had lost his kingdom to a rival Welsh prince, landed from Ireland at Porth Clais, the little harbour below St Davids. There to meet him, with his full retinue of clerics, was Bishop Sulien, together with Rhys ap Tewdwr, king of South Wales, who had sought sanctuary at St Davids, having also lost his kingdom. The two princes, having made a pact on the relics at St Davids, joined forces, fought and defeated their enemies and recovered their kingdoms. This success was clearly not lost upon William.

After their arrival, the Normans took control of many important churches, bestowing them to the great continental monastic houses. Although St Davids remained a bishopric, Wilfrid, Sulien's successor, found himself at the mercy of similar, but unofficial, depredations. Marauding Norman lords seized Church lands for themselves, and also gave them to monastic houses in Britain and on the Continent. In 1115, Henry I, the Conqueror's son, having waited for Wilfrid to die, imposed his own man, Bernard, a former Chancellor to his queen, Mathilda.

In his 33 years as Bishop, Bernard laid the foundations of the modern diocesan and parochial system. Clearly a man of vision and energy, he not only put the diocese in order, but reorganized the clergy of the cathedral into a chapter of secular canons, which still exists today. Yet, for all his drive, Bernard moved carefully. At the time of his arrival, the cathedral was an episcopal mother church, administered, governed and probably owned by a semi-monastic community of hereditary canons, known in Welsh as a *clas* (from the Latin *classis*, a body of people). Yet the creation of the chapter only occurred when the new cathedral was dedicated in 1131. No traces of that church remain, but it is thought to have been where the eastern part of the present building stands. Although it seems that Bernard under-endowed his chapter by giving too much property to Norman lords, he clearly absorbed the traditions and attitudes of his adopted Church with remarkable enthusiasm.

The new cathedral was evidence of this. Its very existence at St Davids was highly significant, for it lay in the remote south-western corner of a huge medieval diocese, stretching 80 miles (130 kilometres) north and east, and inland to the Herefordshire border. The decision not to move to a more central location must have been based on the connection of Dewi with the area and the site.

At the same time as Bernard was attempting to create diocesan structures, his neighbours, the bishops of Hereford and Llandaff, were engaged in the same activity. The issue of borders led to conflict. Llandaff's chief saint is St Teilo, to whom many churches within the see of St Davids were dedicated. Urban, bishop of Llandaff, wished these to come under his jurisdiction. If Bernard had given way, his diocese would not just have been decimated, but would have been uncontrollable. Much prestige and status was at stake as well as money, lands and power. Fortunately, for the future of the St Davids diocese, Bernard won.

In the Middle Ages, the Bishop of St Davids was a Lord Marcher, that is, he held the lands of his episcopate directly from the king but with almost royal rights himself. This power and wealth is reflected in the quality of architecture and decoration both in the cathedral

▼ The view from the south-west. In its valley setting, St Davids
Cathedral enjoys a unique pastoral surrounding, a constant
source of delight to those who see it for the first time.

and also in the 14th-century Bishops' Palace. The decision to keep the symbolic centre of the diocese at St Davids meant that, presumably, Bernard, like his successors, had more than one palace and moved from one to the other on progress, as did secular lords and princes. Bernard was not, however, totally successful in his reforms. He failed, for example, to secure metropolitan status for his diocese. More seriously, having built a new cathedral based primarily on the cult of David, he had one problem: he did not have the corporeal relics of David.

In the medieval period, relics were important. Pilgrims made a difficult journey to a shrine, kneeling in prayer to ask the saint to intercede for them on the Day of Judgement. The belief grew that coming to St Davids or other shrines would earn remission in purgatory, thought to be where the souls of the dead suffer for their sins before going to heaven. Pilgrims would offer money at a shrine: and the practical expression of those offerings at St Davids is the cathedral. The possession of relics by a major church – and each tried to get hold of these if they did not already possess them – was to enhance the status of that church by attracting pilgrims, whose offerings would increase its income.

At Llandaff, Urban succeeded in getting hold of the relics of St Dyfrig and built a new cathedral to hold them. Bernard built a cathedral but, as it were, had nothing to put in it. Medieval commentators say that he spent most of his episcopate looking for David's bones but could not find them. The task should have been simple, since the Life says that David was buried in his own monastery. However, the memory was presumably lost when successive communities were scattered, or even wiped out, by the Vikings. Despite failing to find the relics, Bernard apparently persuaded Pope Calixtus II to give him a privilege, which said that for pilgrims to journey to St Davids twice was the spiritual equivalent of going to Rome once. Thus began pilgrimages to St Davids.

That pilgrims came at all in the 12th and early 13th centuries is somewhat curious, for not only were David's bones not there, but neither were any items

▲ THE STONE BASE OF THE SHRINE OF ST DAVID, ERECTED IN 1275 AND SLIGHTED IN 1538.

associated with him. Such objects – his bell, staff, gospel book and portable altar – were still in existence in the 12th century but at churches in the diocese other than the cathedral, and were said to carry within them the virtues and power of the saint and thus oaths and solemn compacts would be sworn on them. In this vital respect, the situation remained unsatisfactory. For all Bernard's attempts, the cathedral had to wait for John de Gamage, a 13th-century Prior of Ewenni in Glamorgan, to solve the problem. It is said that he had a dream telling him to go and dig so many paces, either from the south gate or from the south door of St Davids Cathedral – the records are ambiguous – and he would find the body of David. So this was done, and what was assumed to be the saint's body was discovered. It was housed in the new shrine of 1275. The relics of David and Justinian were kept in a portable shrine or feretory, which may have rested on the stone table. Above this was a painted timber coving which survived the slighting of the shrine in 1538, as did the mural paintings of St David, St Patrick and St Denis of France in the niches. Below the stone table there were stone receptacles for the alms of pilgrims kneeling before the shrine, offerings reflected in the fine quality of the medieval furnishings and fittings.

▲ An example of chevron moulding on an arch of the 12th-century nave arcade.

BUILDING THE CATHEDRAL: GIRALDUS CAMBRENSIS

Bernard's successor as Bishop was David Fitzgerald, a descendant of Rhys ap Tewdwr, the last king of native South Wales (died 1093). Although his episcopate was comparatively undistinguished, it was he who brought to the cathedral a leading figure in its history, his nephew, Giraldus de Barri, later known as Giraldus Cambrensis (Gerald the Welshman; 1147–1223). Giraldus was a prolific author, which is how so much is known about his life, times and career. We also know that, in return for being dispensed by the Pope from going on crusade, he and Peter de Leia (Bishop 1176–98) were charged with building the present cathedral. Able and bright, Giraldus was the great-grandson of Rhys ap Tewdwr, but also grandson of Gerald of Windsor, a Norman lord in Wales, a potent heredity.

After education in Gloucester and the University of Paris, he came back to Wales full of all the reforming ideas of the 12th-century Church. There he found, to his horror, that the Archdeacon of Brecon had a wife, complained about it, and was made Archdeacon of Brecon (and thus a canon of the cathedral) himself. But that is the only major ecclesiastical dignity he ever had, when he so desperately wanted to be Archbishop of St Davids in an independent Church of Wales.

On three occasions – on his uncle's death and twice afterwards – Giraldus was actually elected Bishop of St Davids, but neither King Henry II nor King John would confirm the appointment. To put someone as nakedly ambitious and potentially powerful as he was, with his Welsh-Norman heredity, in charge of a large important diocese would have been unwise. Besides, Giraldus had quarrelled with the Archbishop of Canterbury, Hubert Walter, in the same way that he had quarrelled with so many others. He took his case to Rome, which held up the appointment for several years, but the king would not budge.

The many books and letters that Giraldus wrote cast him in a rather pathetic light. They include all the visions he had to show that he would become Bishop. One book is called *De Rebus a se Gestis* (The Things That He Did). And yet, in his own terms he never accomplished what he set out to do and to be. Giraldus ended up in retirement in the diocese of Lincoln, where he died around 1223. His most lasting memorial may be the present cathedral building.

▲ A CAPITAL SITUATED IN THE NAVE ARCADE, WITH TRUMPET MOULDING AND FLEUR-DE-LIS.

▼ A MODERN STATUE OF GIRALDUS DE BARRI (GIRALDUS CAMBRENSIS; 1147–1223) IN HOLY TRINITY CHAPEL. AS ARCHDEACON OF BRECON, GIRALDUS PLAYED A MAJOR PART, WITH BISHOP PETER DE LEIA, IN THE BUILDING OF THE CATHEDRAL.

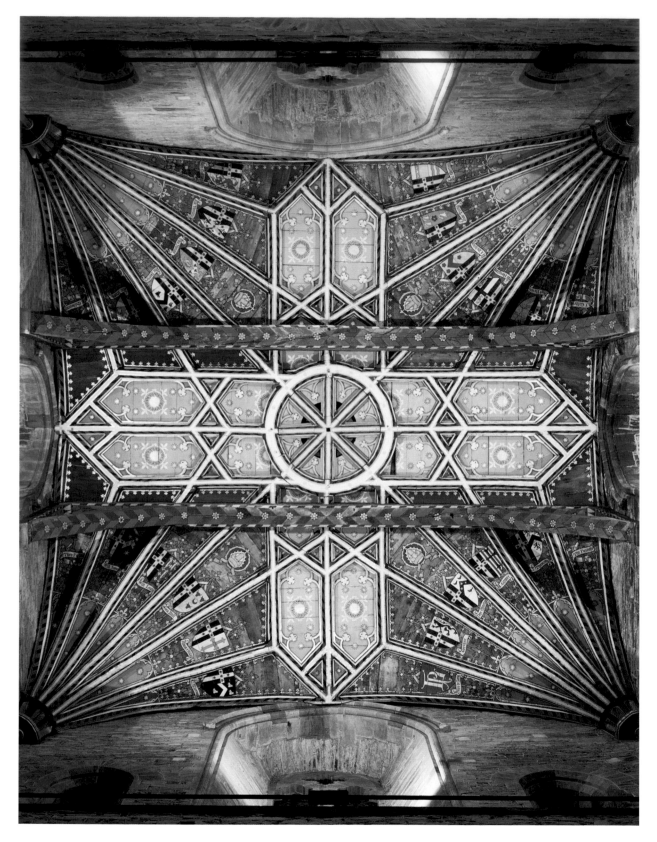

▲ THE TOWER LANTERN. THE COLOURING AND COATS OF ARMS DATE FROM
SCOTT'S RESTORATION. THE TIE-RODS HE INSERTED CAN BE SEEN TOP AND BOTTOM.

THE STRUCTURE

The present cathedral was begun sometime between 1180 and 1182. The Chronicle states that around then 'the church of Menevia was demolished, and the "new work" was begun'. A great deal of that 'new work' survives in the present structure. Much of the cathedral is built in a fine-grained sandstone which was quarried from the cliffs at Caerbwdi, a few miles to the south-east. Inside, the stone has lasted well, protected from the weather but also helped by the murals of the Middle Ages (see page 40) and the regular whitewashing it received between the 17th and 19th centuries.

An impression of the 1182 church can be gained from the nave with its six-bay arcade of alternating round and octagonal pillars, surmounted by heavy

▲ THIS VIEW FROM THE SOUTH-WEST SHOWS THE THREE STAGES OF THE TOWER AND THE PRESSURE PLATES OF SCOTT'S TIE-RODS.

semi-circular arches. Above these, a pair of small pointed arches forms a light stone screen in place of a triforium. This conjunction of round and pointed forms reminds us that the cathedral is a Transitional Romanesque building, its master masons moving towards the Early English style. The building was quite old-fashioned for the 1180s, compared, for example, with Wells Cathedral, built at about the same time in the new Gothic style. The work has affinities with churches on the Welsh borders, shown not only by a similarity of style but through the distinctive marks left by masons to identify their craftsmanship.

Three peculiarities visible in the nave demonstrate the difficulties of the topography and give some hint of

▲ THREE PECULIARITIES IN THE STRUCTURE OF THE NAVE – ITS SLOPE TOWARDS THE WEST END; THE LEAN OF
THE PILLARS; THE FACT THAT THE LAST PAIR OF ARCHES AT THE WEST END IS NEITHER ROUND NOR POINTED –
ALL HINT AT THE COMPLEXITY OF ITS HISTORY. ALSO VISIBLE IS THE FINE 16TH-CENTURY CEILING.

▲ THE ORGAN ATOP BISHOP GOWER'S SCREEN WAS RESTORED IN 2001.
THE ROOD HANGING FROM THE CEILING WAS DESIGNED IN 1931 BY W.D. CAROE.
THE CAROE PARTNERSHIP HAVE BEEN ARCHITECTS TO THE CATHEDRAL FOR OVER A CENTURY.

▲ THE CONJUNCTION OF ROUND ARCHES OF THE NAVE AND CLERESTORY AND THE POINTED ARCHES OF THE TRIFORIUM PROVIDES FURTHER EVIDENCE THAT THE CATHEDRAL IS BUILT IN A STYLE THAT IS TRANSITIONAL BETWEEN ROMANESQUE AND EARLY ENGLISH GOTHIC.

previous buildings on the site. Firstly, the floor slopes in two directions, most markedly from the screen to the west door. The east and west ends of the whole building differ in height by around 14 feet (4 metres). Why did the masons not level the ground before building? The answer is, perhaps, that there may well have been several buildings beyond the east end of the new construction, with which the new work was intended to link up. These would have been in continuous use, making levelling impossible. Instead, the builders took up the gradient by making the nave pillars progressively longer towards the west end, while keeping the arches horizontal. Secondly, the arcades depart quite considerably from the vertical. The explanation for this has been revealed by modern borings, which show that the nave is built on the gravel of an old river bed, making it unstable from the outset. A third unusual feature is that the last pair of arches at the west end is neither round nor pointed. It is possible that the outer walls of the building were built around the previous structure, which was probably east of the present choir screen. This would have allowed continuity of services, and lend significance to the statement in the Chronicle that the church of Menevia was demolished. It is suggested that, because the outer walls were laid out first, the masons, in building the arcading from east to west, miscalculated the spacings. Another suggestion relates to the earthquake of *c.*1247, known to have seriously damaged the cathedral. As a result, the west wall may have been rebuilt inwards of its previous line, which would account for the odd configuration of the arches.

▲ A very early example from the eastern nave arches of
a Green Man – decorative rather than implying any link
with woodland deities.

The nave aisles of the 12th-century cathedral were much lower than those there today, with steeply pitched roofs protecting tribunes – long, low attics. The aisles were lit by small round-headed windows. But in the 14th century Bishop Gower wanted to let in more light.

To accommodate the larger windows that were necessary, the side walls were raised and the pitch of the roof consequently altered. The attics disappeared. The double-rimmed porthole window at the south-west corner bears witness to the change.

◀ THE BLOCKED SPACE BELOW THE
WHEEL WINDOW OF THE SOUTH-
WEST CORNER IS A LEGACY OF A
FORMER WINDOW BELONGING TO
THE LOW 12TH-CENTURY AISLES,
WHICH WERE RAISED BY BISHOP
GOWER IN THE 14TH CENTURY TO
ADMIT MORE LIGHT.

▶ THE ROMANESQUE NORTH
DOOR. BEYOND ARE THE FLYING
BUTTRESSES ERECTED FROM THE LATE
MIDDLE AGES TO SUPPORT THE
NORTH WALL OF THE NAVE.

In past centuries the interior of the cathedral looked very different from the way it looks today. In the Middle Ages, all the interior walls were rendered and coloured (as was much of the exterior). Besides this, there were stained-glass windows, often telling Bible stories to folk unable to read. Remnants of the later heraldic glass can be seen in the north aisle. Many pillars were decorated with murals. In the south nave aisle a mural of King Henry IV is visible, and there are traces of murals on other pillars. Today's nave is arranged for congregational worship, but in the Middle Ages it was absolutely empty. Cathedral naves were built to accommodate processions under cover – nothing else. The only seating from that time is a pair of stone benches near the west door, with further traces of benches in the walls, reflecting the saying 'The weakest go to the wall'. A three-decker pulpit and a few pews appeared after the 16th century, but, only when the building was restored by Sir George Gilbert Scott in Victorian times, was it fitted out as we see it today.

THE WEST FRONT, AS PARTIALLY REBUILT BY JOHN NASH TO COMBAT WESTWARD MOVEMENT OF THE TOWER. SIR GEORGE GILBERT SCOTT IS STANDING ON THE LEFT OF THE GROUP.

▶ THE WEST FRONT TODAY. NASH'S WORK WAS REFACED BY SCOTT, IN RESPONSE NOT ONLY TO MOVEMENT OF THE FABRIC, BUT ALSO A CHANGE OF TASTE.

Over the years, problems with the foundations have caused all the stonework to move. This was exacerbated by the steep pitch of the 12th-century roof which caused the walls to spread. To counteract this outward thrust, elegant flying buttresses, held up by larger, cruder counterparts outside, were built on the north side of the nave from the 14th century. But the problems did not stop there, for the 5,000-tonne tower was insecure and moving westwards. As a consequence, by the end of the 18th century the west front had shifted out by almost 3 feet (1 metre), and was still moving. The Chapter commissioned John Nash to rebuild it. The present west front was designed by Sir George Gilbert Scott as part of his restoration.

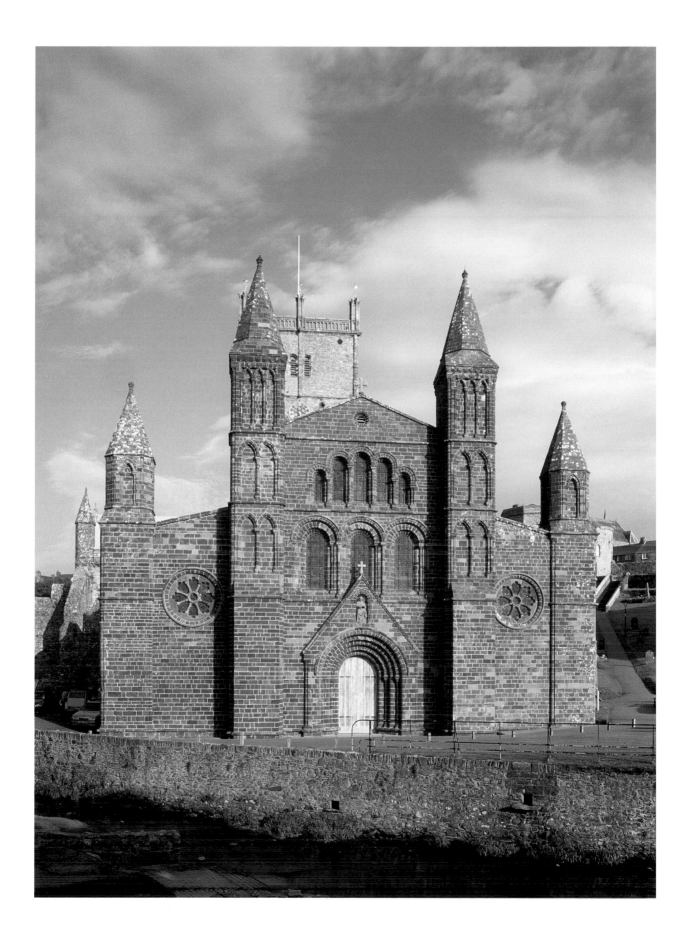

Because of the sloping site and the waterlogged ground, the cathedral's foundations are still shifting. Although the movement is minute, the threat of major damage is never far away. This ever-present insecurity of fabric has meant that, as far as historians can tell, the cathedral has never had stone-vaulted roofs. In the late 15th and early 16th centuries, the nave roof was reconstructed and the splendid, unique, wooden ceiling added. The motifs on its pendants are clearly those of the Renaissance, and the whole is very possibly the work of Flemish or South German craftsmen. The oak is possibly from Ireland, the nearest source, and has been both bleached and preserved by the sea air. Whether it was ever meant to be painted is uncertain. The whole work cost about £400. The ceiling alone cost at least £90, a colossal sum of money at that time. In 1538 Bishop Barlow complained that the canons were using up all their money re-edifying the 'body of the church' which was 'ruinous'! A happy modern addition to the cathedral is the splendid hanging rood, designed by W.D. Caroe, carved by Nathaniel Hitch and hung in the nave in 1931.

◀ THE HANGING ROOD, DONATED ANONYMOUSLY TO THE CATHEDRAL IN 1931, WAS DESIGNED BY W.D. CAROE AND CARVED BY NATHANIEL HITCH.

▼ THE CEILING PENDANTS COMBINE MEDIEVAL AND RENAISSANCE MOTIFS, AND ARE LIKELY TO BE THE WORK OF FLEMISH OR SOUTH GERMAN CRAFTSMEN.

▲ THE UNIQUE OAK CEILING WAS CREATED IN THE 16TH CENTURY, A HAPPY
EXPEDIENT BECAUSE A STONE VAULT WOULD NOT HAVE BEEN POSSIBLE.

▲ A 13TH-CENTURY CARVED HEAD FROM THE ANTECHAPEL, ONE OF THE 'SEVEN BEAUTIES OF SOUTH WALES'.

MONUMENT TO A BISHOP

Medieval churches were not wide open spaces where one sat and listened to sermons; that is a post-Reformation concept. Rather they were a series of chambers, large or small, with distinctive functions, separated by stone or wooden screens. The massive stone screen between presbytery and nave was erected by Henry Gower, Bishop (1328–47), partially, at least, to house his tomb. Late Decorative Gothic in style, it was the base for both the rood and the rood loft. It is thought to consist of two parts, the northern side being an earlier screen that Gower brought forward when he constructed the new screen. Gower did much in the cathedral, but the epitaph on his tomb, until it was taken away by Parliamentary soldiers, read 'Here lies Henry Gower, constructor of the Palace', which he clearly considered to be his greatest achievement.

▼ WITHIN THE SOUTHERN COMPARTMENT OF THE SCREEN IS THE TOMB OF HENRY GOWER, BISHOP 1328–47, WHO BUILT THE STRUCTURE PARTLY AS HIS FINAL RESTING PLACE.

▼ The screen. Beneath the present organ are sockets which
indicate that it once carried a standing rood, removed in
1571. The timber parapet contains work of the 16th, 19th
and 20th centuries.

▲ The cathedral from the west, viewed across the great hall of the Bishops' Palace, built by Bishop Gower to entertain distinguished guests who had come as pilgrims.

◀ A 12th-century bishop's crozier, perhaps that of Richard de Carew, recovered during Sir George Gilbert Scott's restoration.

▶ An aerial view of the cathedral and the 14th-century Bishops' Palace, with Porth-y-Twr and the modern city of St Davids beyond.

▲ The lion of St Mark, a medieval painting from within the screen, preserved for centuries beneath whitewash.

▲ On the inner arch of the screen: an owl being taunted by magpies – wisdom mocked by foolishness.

The dais before the screen is one of the original 12th-century features of the nave. Under its pavement are the graves of at least three bishops. These are probably Peter de Leia, who built the 1182 cathedral, Thomas Bec, (died 1293), and Richard de Carew, (died 1280). The figures on the front of the screen are modern (1909–17): on the north side, Our Lord, flanked by St John and St Paul; on the south side, St David. The dove from the legend is on his shoulder. Nearby, an attractive banner from the 1980s shows David with the ground rising beneath his feet, again reflecting what was said to have happened at Llanddewi Brefi. The central passage linking the nave with the presbytery is flanked by two tomb spaces. The roof of the one on the north side has remarkable 14th-century murals depicting the symbols of the four evangelists, a crucifixion scene and, it is thought, the reception of a soul into heaven. Nearby is an owl being mocked by magpies – wisdom being mocked by foolishness. The murals' survival is all the more remarkable because their surfaces were once whitewashed, and, at one time, the passage was blocked in order to help stop the tower from collapsing.

The timber above the stone screen is of different dates. The lower portion is medieval, and was probably part of the rood loft, although irregularity at its base suggests that it was adapted from stall canopies. The portion above it is by William Butterfield and the cornice above by A.D.R. Caroe. On the screen stands the organ. There appears to have been an organ at St Davids from the 14th century onwards, but an instrument rather smaller than the present one, located under the western tower arch and facing the quire. The organ was just one more item destroyed by Parliamentary soldiers in 1648. After this, the chapter commissioned 'Father' Smith to construct a new organ, in place by 1705, which was replaced in 1843 by the Lincoln organ, retaining the Smith case. Both of these organs were located under the north tower arch. In 1883, a new three manual organ was constructed by Henry 'Father' Willis, located on the screen further westwards than the medieval organ, in order to serve both nave and quire. This instrument was re-cased, by A.D.R. Caroe during the 1953 rebuild of the Willis organ, and enhanced and altered in various ways until the major rebuild and re-casing by Harrisons in 2000.

▲ A 14TH-CENTURY CARVED HEAD FROM THE SCREEN, BEAUTIFUL
IN ITS SIMPLICITY OF LINE.

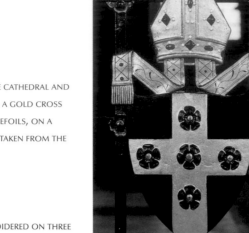

▶ THE COAT OF ARMS OF THE CATHEDRAL AND THE DIOCESE OF ST DAVIDS IS A GOLD CROSS ADORNED WITH BLACK CINQUEFOILS, ON A BLACK FIELD. THIS EXAMPLE IS TAKEN FROM THE GATES OF THE ANTECHAPEL.

▶ ORGANS HAVE DOMINATED THE QUIRE IN VARIOUS POSITIONS SINCE THE 14TH CENTURY. THE CURRENT ONE, THE FIRST TO SERVE BOTH QUIRE AND NAVE, DATES FROM 1883. NOTE THE PROJECTION OF THE PARAPET TO ACCOMMODATE THE ORGANIST IN MEDIEVAL TIMES.

▼ THE COAT OF ARMS EMBROIDERED ON THREE COPES, MADE IN 1974.

THE QUIRE

Beyond the screen lie the quire and the presbytery, the heart of the cathedral. Here stands the *cathedra,* or throne, of the Bishop of St Davids. It was probably constructed by Bishop Gower in the 14th century. Almost 29 feet (9 metres) high, it was once decorated with angels and saints, which can still be seen above the central seat. The governance of an Anglican cathedral is delegated by a bishop to a body of clerics known as a Dean and Chapter, and St Davids is blessed with a magnificent set of 16th-century stalls beneath the tower as seating for the members of the chapter. Several features are worthy of note: the carvings on the bench

◄ ▲ THE MAGNIFICENT BISHOP'S THRONE (OR 'CATHEDRA') WAS CARVED FOR BISHOP GOWER IN THE 14TH CENTURY. ABOVE IS A DETAIL OF THE ELABORATE WORK. THE THRONE WAS MOVED WESTWARDS TO ITS PRESENT PLACE IN THE 16TH CENTURY, DISPLACING THE PARCLOSE SCREEN.

▼ A CANOPY OVER THE CENTRAL EPISCOPAL SEAT WAS DECORATED
WITH PAINTINGS OF SAINTS, BISHOPS AND ANGELS, TRACES OF
WHICH STILL REMAIN.

▲ ▼ ▶ THE STALLS DATE FROM THE EARLY 16TH CENTURY. THIS CAN BE DEDUCED FROM THREE CARVED BENCH ENDS WITH LINKS TO THE PERIOD: THE TUDOR ROSE (TOP), THE POMEGRANATE (BELOW) AND THE PRINCE OF WALES'S FEATHERS (RIGHT). THE POMEGRAN-ATE (THE APPLE OF GRANADA) IS A PUN ON THE NAME OF CATHERINE OF ARAGON, WHO MARRIED FIRST PRINCE ARTHUR (1501–15) AND THEN HIS BROTHER, SOON TO BE HENRY VIII.

▶ THE STALLS HAVE A VERY FINE SERIES OF CARVED MISERICORDS. THIS EXAMPLE SHOWS SEASICKNESS.

ends, the original coats of arms which survive in six
stalls, the small carved faces amid the tracery behind
the stalls, and the stalls themselves with their misericords, medieval tip-up seats designed to take the weight
off the feet of clergy forced to stand for long periods.
The names on the back of the stalls are those of the
prebends, churches or manors once owned by the
chapter and which, before the disestablishment of the
Church in Wales, provided the income for the
prebendary or canon who sat there. Clergy seating at
St Davids has several features peculiar to itself: the
Dean sits on the north side, where the Precentor would
normally sit; the Bishop has a stall in the quire where
the Dean should be; and for unknown reasons, there is
a stall for the reigning sovereign. Queen Elizabeth II has
sat there four times: in 1955; in 1982 when she distrib-
uted the Royal Maundy at St Davids; in 1995 when she
gave city status back to St Davids; and in 2001.

◀ THE CHAPTER BADGE. UNIQUELY
IN BRITAIN, THE REIGNING
SOVEREIGN IS A MEMBER OF
THE CATHEDRAL CHAPTER.

▼ THE CUSHION FROM THE ROYAL
STALL IN THE QUIRE, BEARING THE
ROYAL COAT OF ARMS.

▲ A CUSHION FROM THE DEAN'S STALL, MADE BY THE
EMBROIDERY GUILD OF THE CATHEDRAL.

▲ ▶ THE STALLS FOR CLERGY AND CHOIR PROVIDE A RICH SHOWCASE FOR THE CARVER'S ART. THE ARMS AND BACKS OF THE STALLS INCLUDE OVER 60 FACES.

High above the quire, the western arch of the tower is round-headed, while the other three are pointed. This is a reminder that the tower collapsed in 1220, and, when it was rebuilt, it was in the more modern Gothic style, except, unwisely, for the western arch. In the 14th century, Bishop Gower added the middle stage of the tower, known as the lantern because it lets in light. The third and upper stage dates probably to the episcopate of Edward Vaughan, Bishop 1509–22. The western arch had to be rebuilt by Scott in the 1860s. Still unsound from the earthquake of 1247, it had for centuries to bear the weight of Gower's additions. Things were made worse by a troop of Cromwell's dragoons in 1648. With puritanical zeal, they smashed the stained-glass windows, stripped the lead from the roof, ripped brasses from tombs, burned books and removed at least one of the bells, making a large breach in the south face of the tower to do so. When Scott was called in, the tower was in a parlous condition. He rebuilt it all, furnishing foundations where none had existed before and inserting tie-rods to hold it together. Nevertheless, in 1931 it was judged unwise to place a new ring of bells in the central tower; instead they were set in the original 13th-century detached bell tower adjacent to Porth-y-Tŵr. Since 1865, the central tower has been largely sound, and this has to some extent stopped the movement in the rest of the building.

▲ Porth-y-Tŵr as seen from the cathedral tower. Since 1931 the bells once more ring there, as they did in the 13th century.

▲ The Succentor's stall, with a
misericord depicting a country dance.

◄ Often seen but seldom noticed:
one of the pinnacles of the tower,
decorated by ornate beasts, placed
there by Sir George Gilbert Scott.

▶ Morning sunlight emphasizes the
beauty of the carved frieze behind the
high altar and the rich texture of the
natural stone beneath. The wall below
may be part of the church of 1131.

THE PRESBYTERY

The presbytery, very evidently, has had a complex building history. Its alternating round and octagonal piers appear to be early 13th-century, while the central circular piers look earlier. Moreover, the arches of the arcades belong to a scheme different from that of the piers, and the variety of vaulting shafts attached to the front of the piers indicate many changes of intention, not least as to whether a stone vault was to be constructed. In the event, the raising of the side walls 5 feet (1.5 metres), in preparation for a camber-beam roof in the late 15th or early 16th century, made the issue of the vault irrelevant. The east wall of the presbytery represents many periods and many changes. Two much-debated, yet unlikely, theories are that the base of the east wall belongs to the church of 1131, and that the opening behind the high altar linked to the niche in Holy Trinity Chapel relates to the site of the original shrine. As part of this complex and intractable puzzle, the splendid banded lancet windows of 1220 do not conform with the walls below or around them; indeed, halfway up the wall there is a very clear change of build. Sir George Gilbert Scott in his restoration of 1863–1901 attempted to preserve features which were archaeologically important. His work in the presbytery bears this out for, in pursuit of this aim, he reconstructed the quadruple lancets, taking out the large 16th-century

▲ A MOSAIC DETAIL FROM BEHIND THE HIGH ALTAR.

window which had replaced them. As the main triple lancets behind the high altar were necessarily blocked following the construction of Holy Trinity Chapel, Scott installed fine mosaics, designed by Hardman's (who also furnished the glass for the quadruple lancets) and executed by Salviati. On the floor on the south side of the presbytery are two effigies of earlier bishops: Anselm le Gras and Iorwerth, who in 1215 became the first Welsh Bishop of St Davids for over a century. He was the author of the oldest surviving set of statutes that the cathedral possesses. Nearby, lies Rhys ap Gruffydd, the Lord Rhys, a significant figure of late 12th-century Wales and a great benefactor to the cathedral. In the next bay to the east lies an effigy often described as being that of Giraldus Cambrensis, but is much more likely to be that of his nephew, Giraldus Fitzphilip de Barri.

The late 15th and early 16th centuries saw major developments throughout the cathedral: flying buttresses in the north aisle, new choir stalls, the shifting of the bishop's throne eastwards, the parclose screen, the presbytery and nave ceilings and, finally, the construction of the tomb of Edmund Tudor, Earl of Richmond (died 1456), whose body was moved, at the Dissolution, from its original burial place in the church of the Greyfriars in Carmarthen. His epitaph states that

▼ THE PRESBYTERY. CENTRALLY, BEYOND THE PARCLOSE SCREEN, IS THE
TOMB OF EDMUND TUDOR, AND TO THE LEFT IS THE BASE OF ST DAVID'S
SHRINE. THE CEILING WAS RECOLOURED IN SCOTT'S RESTORATION.

▲ BEHIND THE HIGH ALTAR ARE WINDOWS RENDERED 'BLIND' WHEN THE HOLY TRINITY CHAPEL WAS CREATED IN THE 16TH CENTURY. IN THE SPACES SCOTT INSTALLED MOSAICS, DESIGNED BY HARDMAN AND MADE BY SALVIATI, DEPICTING SCENES FROM THE LIFE OF DAVID.

▶ A CARVED ANGEL FROM THE 16TH-CENTURY SEDILIA IN THE PRESBYTERY. THE CATHEDRAL BOASTS MANY SUCH DETAILS – EXQUISITE, BUT EASY TO MISS BECAUSE OF THEIR SIZE.

he was 'father and brother to kings', for Edmund was the father of King Henry VII and the half-brother of King Henry VI. The brass on the tomb is a copy of that stripped off by Cromwell's men in the 1640s. The tomb stands in a very awkward position in terms of services at the high altar, but relates to its location at Carmarthen. It may also express an attempt to draw attention away from St David's shrine nearby, a symbol of the old order. Its arrival coincided with the early years of the episcopate of William Barlow, the first Protestant Bishop of St Davids (1536–47). To break the hold of the 'old religion' Barlow wished to remove both cathedral and palace to Carmarthen, as an urban, more Anglicized, less conservative part of the diocese. He failed. The cathedral remained at St Davids and Edmund Tudor was brought there. The bishop's main residence did move to Carmarthen, however. Edmund Tudor's presence at St Davids is thought to have proved useful in persuading Henry VIII not to close the cathedral because his grandfather was buried here. The same argument, it seems, persuaded Charles II not to allow a later bid to transfer cathedral status to Carmarthen. It took one of Barlow's successors, Richard Davies, the great Elizabethan Bishop of St David's (1561–81) to suggest that for the Reformation to succeed in the diocese of St Davids and Wales generally, it had to be introduced and established through the medium of Welsh. Davies oversaw legislation which by 1588 had brought about the translation of the Prayer Book and the Bible into Welsh.

In medieval times, the area was an important element in controlling the large numbers of pilgrims circulating through the building, and it is said that the ancient tiles which once paved the floor by St David's shrine bore grooves worn by the knees of the pilgrims. Similarly, tradition has it that the hoofmarks of Cromwell's horsemen could still be seen from that fateful August day in 1648. Today's presbytery floor was laid as part of Scott's Victorian restoration. However the tiles inside the altar rail are 16th-century, gathered from the rest of the building by Scott. The splendid sedilia too is 16th-century, miraculously having escaped the attentions of the Roundheads and the decay of subsequent years.

▲ THE TOMB OF EDMUND TUDOR, EARL OF RICHMOND (DIED 1456), WHO WAS THE FATHER OF KING HENRY VII AND THE HALF-BROTHER OF KING HENRY VI.

Thanks to the depredations of Cromwell's men, by the mid-17th century the presbytery, and indeed most of the cathedral, was in a parlous state. The presbytery arches were blocked with solid walls, the aisles beyond being open to the sky; all the roofs at the east end were off and all the lead had been stripped from the roof of the Lady Chapel, which was to collapse in 1775.

▲ ONE OF A SERIES OF CLIENT DRAWINGS BY NASH'S DRAUGHTSMAN, AUGUSTIN PUGIN, SHOWING THE DILAPIDATED STATE WHICH THE CATHEDRAL HAD REACHED BY THE 18TH CENTURY.

▼ A PHOTOGRAPH OF THE CATHEDRAL TAKEN SHORTLY BEFORE 1897. ITS PARTICULAR INTEREST LIES IN THE THEN ROOFLESS LADY CHAPEL SEEN TO THE RIGHT, AND ALSO IN PUGIN'S DRAWING ABOVE.

THE EAST END

Just as a burst of activity in the late 12th century had built the cruciform cathedral, so, in the 13th century, the cathedral experienced major extension and renovation. Early in that century, the authorities created an ambulatory, or covered walkway, beyond the north and south quire aisles to help manage the great numbers of pilgrims, who came even before the body of David was discovered, and which acts as an antechapel to the Lady Chapel. The Lady Chapel has fine 14th-century sedilia and tombs, now restored. However, after 1648, centuries without lead on its roof left it in ruins, until restoration in 1901.

▲ THIS SPACE, NOW AN ANTECHAPEL TO THE LADY CHAPEL, BEGAN LIFE IN THE 13TH CENTURY AS AN AMBULATORY FOR PILGRIMS.

▼ The Lady Chapel, roofless and abandoned for centuries, was restored in 1901. The Welsh-speaking congregation worships here on Sundays.

▶ This fine alloy and glass screen was created by Frank Roper in 1979 as an entrance to the Lady Chapel.

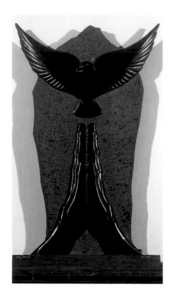

▶ Praying Hands, by local sculptor Reg Beach, located in a 13th-century window space in the south wall of the Lady Chapel.

The Lady Chapel was begun in the late 13th century and completed in the 14th as a five- or six-bay chapel. It may have originally been a detached building, perhaps a 'well chapel', for it is slightly offline from the main cathedral, and the holy well is located just beyond the east wall. In the 16th century it was remodelled into a Perpendicular two-bay building, raising the walls of the antechapel by 10 feet (3 metres). Today the cathedral's Welsh congregation meets there for Sunday worship. The south chapel aisle, the last part of the ruined east end to be restored, was re-roofed in 1907. The fittings were donated in the 1920s by the Countess of Maidstone (died 1932), who is buried in the north-eastern corner in an elaborately carved alabaster tomb.

◀ A statue of the Madonna and Child on the eastern gable end of the Lady Chapel, dating from the 1901 restoration.

▶ The powerful limestone effigy of John Owen, bishop 1897–1926, from his tomb in the Lady Chapel, designed by W.D. Caroe.

▲ THE CHAPEL OF ST EDWARD THE CONFESSOR. THE FITTINGS WERE
DONATED IN THE 1920S BY THE COUNTESS OF MAIDSTONE, WHOSE
TOMB IS IN THE NORTH-EASTERN CORNER (VISIBLE CENTRE). HER GRAND-
FATHER, JOHN BANKS JENKINSON, WAS BISHOP OF ST DAVIDS BETWEEN
1825 AND 1840.

▶ A FINELY WORKED DETAIL FROM THE ALABASTER CARVING OF THE
CHAPEL'S REREDOS SHOWS ONE OF THE FOUR 'LIVING BEASTS' FROM
THE BOOK OF REVELATION.

Contained within the space defined by the ambulatory lies Holy Trinity Chapel. Edward Vaughan, (Bishop 1509–22), had this previously filthy area beyond the east end cleared – it cost him 4 pence, a large sum of money for the time – so that he might prepare his own burial place and to create a chantry chapel there. The chapel is Perpendicular in style, with a splendid fan-vaulted ceiling. It was restored very effectively in 1923, and is used regularly during the week for early morning services and the Eucharist, as are the other chapels in the cathedral. The unusual altar was created by W.D. Caroe from fragments of early Christian monuments, medieval stonework and the original altar slab. Opposite the altar, the niche in the old exterior east wall of the cathedral connects with the area behind the high altar. From perhaps as early as 1522, maybe even earlier, it was walled up and plastered over, but opened up during Scott's restoration in 1865. Amongst the items revealed was a large number of bones, at the time considered unimportant. Theories about the niche vary. The Victorians thought it was a place where pilgrims could gain access to a shrine or relics on the site of the present high altar. However there is no evidence for a shrine of David in the building before 1275.

▲ A detail from the fine Perpendicular fan vaulting of Holy Trinity Chapel. The coat of arms is that of King Henry VII.

▲ ◀ The altar of Holy Trinity Chapel and, inset, a 14th-century detail from the reredos depicting St James, patron saint of pilgrims. The altar is a masterly reconstruction of medieval fragments.

▶ THIS STONE FIGURE FROM AN EXTERNAL CORNER HIGH UP ON THE ANTECHAPEL MAY BE THAT OF AN UNKNOWN 16TH-CENTURY MASTER MASON, OR ARCHITECT.

In the 1920s, the Dean of the time, William Williams, without any proof, convinced himself that the bones found in the wall were those of David and Justinian, rescued from the destruction of the shrine in 1538 and hidden away here. He had them placed in the casket we see today. Carbon dating has since proved him wrong, the bones being from the 12th, 13th and 14th centuries. In any case, in a surviving letter to Thomas Cromwell, Bishop Barlow points out that he had warned the chapter that they were not to expose the relics of David on 1st March 1538. They defied him and the bones with their accompanying reliquaries were seized.

▲ THE CASKET CONTAINING BONES ONCE THOUGHT TO BE THOSE OF DAVID AND JUSTINIAN.

▲ THE EAST END OF THE CATHEDRAL. THE THREE-STOREY WING ON THE SOUTH SIDE COMPRISES THE LIBRARY WITH BELOW,
ST THOMAS'S CHAPEL. FAR RIGHT IS ST MARY'S HALL.

THE TRANSEPTS

The north transept, apparently featureless, is in fact packed with interest. Its great north window in the Early Perpendicular style was put in by William Butterfield in 1844, as a copy of a window at Sleaford in Lincolnshire. One of the two tombs under the tower arch on the south side is that of Caradog, a 12th-century saint whom Giraldus tried to have canonized but failed. As far as is known, his relics are still in the tomb. The centre bay of the north transept is St Andrew's Chapel, which was restored in the 1950s as the Pembrokeshire War Memorial Chapel; it contains the Book of Remembrance, a page of which is turned over every day. Opening out of the north-east corner of the transept is the Chapel of St Thomas Becket, located in the lowest stage of a three-storey structure, above it being the library, formerly the chapter house, with the treasury above. Although the ceiling vault of St Thomas's Chapel is rather rough, the carved bosses are of very high quality. On the south wall is a fine Early English piscina, indicating that there was probably a chapel here about 1220 when St Thomas's remains were moved to a new shrine within Canterbury Cathedral. Henry II came to St Davids to attend Mass in 1171, the year after Becket's murder.

◀ WILLIAM BUTTERFIELD'S FINE PERPENDICULAR-STYLE WINDOW OF 1844, IN THE NORTH TRANSEPT, IS SOMEHOW ENHANCED BY THE RURAL VIEW BEYOND.

▼ THE CHAPEL OF ST THOMAS BECKET IS THE 'GROUND FLOOR' OF THE
THREE STOREYS. IT PROBABLY STANDS ON THE SITE OF 'THE OLD CHURCH
OF ST ANDREW' WHICH STOOD NEXT TO THE CATHEDRAL.
THE STAINED GLASS, ALTAR AND FITTINGS ARE 20TH-CENTURY, WHILE THE
VAULTED CEILING DATES FROM BISHOP GOWER'S TIME. THE PISCINA,
SEEN RIGHT, IS 13TH-CENTURY, AND EARLY ENGLISH IN STYLE.

▲ A SPLENDID 14TH-CENTURY BOSS FROM THE STONE VAULT OF THE CHAPEL OF ST THOMAS BECKET. IT DEPICTS OUR LORD.

▶ THE DRAGON IS ONE OF THE CEILING BOSSES OF ST THOMAS'S CHAPEL; THE BIRD IS CARVED ON THE 13TH-CENTURY PISCINA.

◀ THE CATHEDRAL LIBRARY IS LOCATED IN
WHAT WAS FORMERLY THE MEDIEVAL CHAPTER
HOUSE. ON ITS NORTH SIDE IS THIS SUPERB
PAIR OF WINDOW SEATS WITH, ABOVE THEM,
14TH-CENTURY NODDING OGEE CANOPIES.

▼ THE LIBRARY WAS RESTORED IN 1956
THROUGH THE GENEROSITY OF THE PILGRIM
TRUST AND OTHERS AS A MEMORIAL TO
THOMAS HAVARD (BISHOP 1950–6). ONE OF
ITS NOTABLE FEATURES IS THIS SPLENDID
14TH-CENTURY FIREPLACE WITH, ABOVE IT, A
STONE CHIMNEY IN THE DECORATIVE STYLE.

An interesting peculiarity here is that the so-called 'Pilgrims' Doorway', in the west wall of the north transept, lines up with the altar of St Thomas's Chapel, and both are off-line with the rest of the cathedral. The cathedral is dedicated not just to St David, but also to St Andrew, and there is a strong possibility that the chapel is on the site of what Giraldus called 'the Old Church of St Andrew' which lay next to the cathedral. It seems likely that the transept was thrown across it, cutting the old church in half. Restored in 1956, the chapel is now reserved for private prayer.

The lower stage of the cathedral library above the chapel was the medieval chapter house, where the canons met regularly to conduct the business of the cathedral. The upper gallery of the present library was the treasury, where the cathedral's liturgical plate and books were kept. In the 18th and 19th centuries these two storeys housed the cathedral's grammar school. It was fitted out as a library in the 1950s.

▲ Scott re-tiled much of the cathedral floor. These tiles represent pike (luces), the coat of arms of the Lucy family who were associated with the restoration of the presbytery.

The south transept today houses vestries placed there in the 1950s, but, in 1844, it was furnished as the parish church of St Davids by William Butterfield. Scott's restoration swept it away, and for the first time the whole cathedral served both the parochial congregation and the cathedral foundation. Also in the south transept, the south-east pier of the tower reveals not only the original (and ineffective) support for the tower but also the junction between the original work and the rebuilding after the collapse of 1220. Above that, it is all of one build, and restored by Scott. Under the southern tower arch on the north side of the south transept, lies an organ case designed by A.D.R. Caroe in 1953 to house part of the pedal organ. It now houses the Willis choir organ and the pedal reeds.

◀ The south quire aisle viewed from the south transept. On the left is one of the original tower buttresses.

▶ An icon in the south transept shows Elijah being fed by the ravens, with other scenes from the prophet's life. Given to the cathedral in the 1960s, it came with an elaborate pseudo-history that it had been brought back from the Crusades, kept in a local abbey and sold off at the Dissolution. It is, however, a 17th or 18th-century work, perhaps Cretan or Byzantine in origin.

▲ ONE OF A PAIR OF TRUMPETING ANGELS WHICH SURMOUNT THE PROJECTING ORGAN PARAPET,
A HAPPY MODERN ADDITION TO THE QUIRE FURNISHINGS.

THE CATHEDRAL CLOSE

The 14th-century wall with its 16-foot (5-metre) battlements once surrounded the medieval city of St Davids. This 16-acre (6.5-hectare) close housed the people: clergy and laity who administered, and indeed, still administer, the cathedral. The most prominent building in the Close, besides the cathedral, is the ruined Bishops' Palace, probably the finest domestic building in the whole of western Britain. This magnificent structure has two separate ranges, with a third, less grand, range to the north-

north-west. Many distinguished pilgrims, mostly royalty, followed William the Conqueror to St Davids. Henry II came here twice and had dinner in the predecessor of the present Bishops' Palace, entertained by David Fitzgerald, uncle of Giraldus Cambrensis. The site of this building, where Bishop Bernard and some of his successors lived, is thought to be the little earth-castle or ringwork at Castell Penlan, which can be seen about half a mile (1 kilometre) down the valley from the present cathedral.

▲ THE BISHOPS' PALACE WAS BUILT IN THE 14TH CENTURY BY BISHOP GOWER. IN THE FOREGROUND IS
THE EAST WING, THE BISHOP'S QUARTERS; THE WHEEL WINDOW MARKS ONE END OF THE GREAT HALL.

Edward I came here; Edward III was meant to come here but didn't. However, great statues of Edward and Queen Philippa in the porch on the way into the Great Hall indicate that this was probably built for a royal visit. The second main range includes the bishop's apartments, the hall, the chapel and the solar, with the kitchen in the angle between it and the first range. All of this was built by Bishop Gower in the middle of the 14th century, a splendid construction with polychrome decoration on the walls, and a distinctive chequerboard decoration on the parapet. This rises above the main walls, and made a statement about the Bishop's wealth and power to those coming down the hillside towards the cathedral. Other buildings, such as the Deanery, the Archdeaconries and the Canonry, are 19th century, built on 13th- and 14th-century foundations.

The medieval wall was once pierced by four gates, of which only one now survives. That is Porth-y-Twr which means in Welsh 'the tower gate'. The octagonal portion of this was built to house the cathedral bells when the central tower of the cathedral was two stages lower than it is now. At the same time as Bishop Gower raised the side walls of the aisles and put in the modern fenestration, he heightened the tower and returned the bells to the cathedral. However, since 1931 the bells once more ring from Porth-y-Twr. During the intervening centuries, archives were kept in it, and a gateway built adjacent to it. In 2000 this was re-roofed in order to house, in its upper storey, an exhibition relating to the life of the cathedral.

▲ PORTH-Y-TŴR WAS RE-ROOFED IN 2000 TO ACCOMMODATE THE CATHEDRAL EXHIBITION IN ITS UPPER STOREY.

▼ THE 14TH-CENTURY CLOSE WALL WHICH WAS BUILT TO SURROUND THE MEDIEVAL CITY OF ST DAVIDS.

▲ Porth-y-Tŵr (the Gate of the Tower) is the only medieval gate to survive at St Davids. The 13th-century octagonal tower was built to house the cathedral bells, the gate being added in the 14th century.

▲ THE MEDIEVAL CLOISTER HAD DISAPPEARED BY 1790 AND IS THE LAST PART OF THE CATHEDRAL AWAITING RESTORATION.

▶ ST MARY'S HALL WAS ORIGINALLY ONE OF A CLUSTER OF BUILDINGS HOUSING A MASTER AND SEVEN FELLOWS, A BODY OF CLERICS FOUNDED TO IMPROVE THE STANDARDS OF CATHEDRAL SERVICES.

Adjacent to the cathedral on the north side are the cloister, the cathedral hall and beyond that Cloister Hall. In the late 14th century these were all one complex because a college – in the medieval sense, a group of clergy whose purpose was to raise standards and serve the cathedral – was founded here in honour of the Blessed Virgin Mary for a Master and seven fellows. It was well endowed with churches and manors and, towards the end of its existence, it absorbed the College of Vicars Choral, the body of clerics who sang the choral services of the cathedral.

It was dissolved in 1549 under the Chantries Act. The first-floor vaults of the college survive in their entirety under the garden of Cloister Hall, while the ruins of the College of Vicars Choral lie underneath the north-west quadrant of the green space in the Close. The chapel, built in the early Perpendicular style, was restored and re-roofed in 1966 for use as the cathedral hall. At the time of writing, plans for the restoration of the cloister are in hand. This represents the last part of the cathedral to be restored, following the depreda-tions of the 16th and the 17th centuries.

POSTSCRIPT

The story of St Davids Cathedral is, however, more than the story of its buildings. Here, for almost fifteen centuries, since the time of David himself, worship has been offered up to God in the name of Jesus Christ by a Christian community. Here, generations of the people of St Davids have been baptized in the font, married before the altar and buried in the churchyard; here, pilgrims have sought and found solace and still do so; here, visitors and tourists are drawn, not only by the cultural and historical significance of St Davids, but also by the sheer natural beauty of the area and this remarkable group of buildings clustering in the Merrivale, the name today of that 'marshy valley' (*Vallis Rosina*) to which David came all those centuries ago.

▲ ST DAVIDS CATHEDRAL IS UNIQUE IN THAT THE TREBLE LINE
OF THE CHOIR HAS BEEN SUNG BY GIRLS SINCE THE 1960s.

▼ The candlelit service of Nine Lessons and Carols is only one
of many choral services sung throughout the year.

▲ TWO HEADS, ONE A KNIGHT, THE OTHER A GROTESQUE, CARVED ON
THE ROOD SCREEN.

▲ Concerts play an important part in the life of the cathedral, the highlight of the musical year being the St Davids Festival, held in early summer.

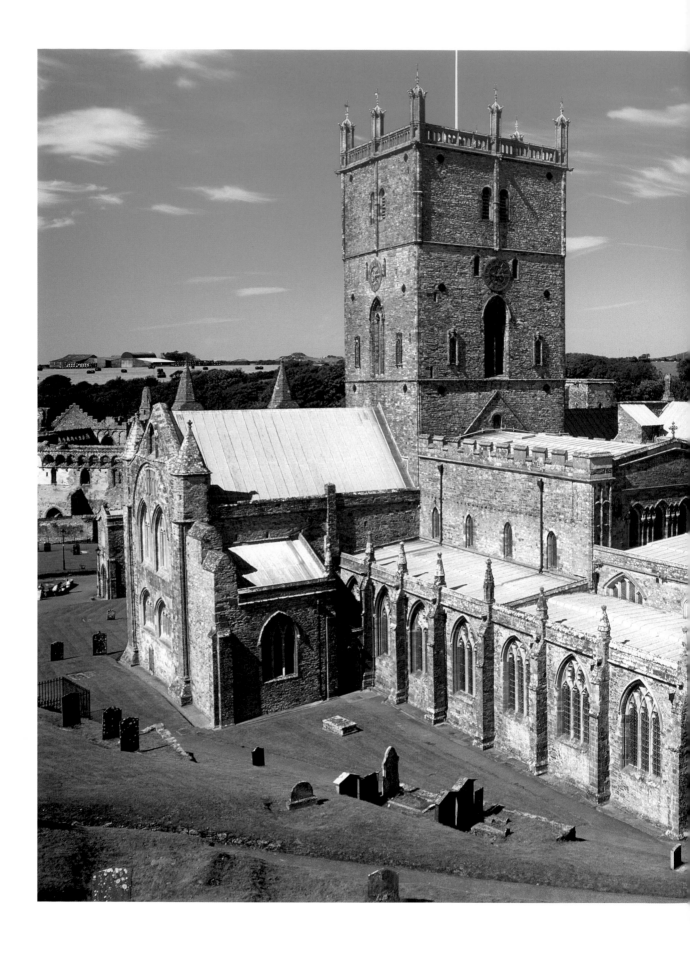

◀ THE CATHEDRAL FROM THE
SOUTH-EAST. THIS CLASSIC VIEW
FROM PORTH-Y-TŴR, ENCOMPASSING
THE BISHOPS' PALACE, THE WOODED
VALLEY OF THE ALUN AND THE ROCKY
OUTCROPS OF THE COAST BEYOND,
DEMONSTRATES AMPLY WHY MANY
THOUSANDS OF VISITORS COME TO
ST DAVIDS EACH YEAR.

INDEX